Ex Libris

Edition **4** No. 402

Jane Beecher Scott

This edition is made possible

through the generous support of –

3M Club Reps and Friends

GBC General Binding Corporation

Wausau Paper

Mosquito Bridge Secret

by Jane Beecher Scott

The story of a wise little mosquito in a quaint little Rivertown who one-by-one talks her predators into moving across the river. It's a lesson in science and life that is sure to delight young and old readers alike.

Preface

osquito Bridge Secret was inspired by a real midwestern river town named Stillwater where the townspeople couldn't decide whether or not to build a new bridge. Some people thought it was a good idea, and just as many others were sure it was the worst idea in the world. They couldn't seem to agree. It became a major debate–the talk of the town in local newspapers, on street corners, in cafes, on radio and TV, the internet and everywhere you turned. What I decided would help was a fresh perspective. This book looks at the new-bridge question from the point of view of another large population besides people that might be affected by a new bridge–namely river town mosquitoes.

That's how this book came to be.

I hope the mosquito sheds a fresh light on the subject for any town that considers building a new bridge–how it might benefit more than just people. And maybe why it might not be such a good idea too. There's two sides to every story. But one thing almost everyone would generally agree with is that, in many ways at least, it's better to build bridges than walls.

Grapevine Arachnid

It's autumn and the grapes are just starting to change color and get plump on the vines. In a sunny spot behind the winery, deep in a cluster of grapes, lives a pale green arachnid. He matches the color of the leaves. Before the grapes ripened and turned purple, he matched them too.

His eight legs cling tightly to the lace clusters of ripe fruit, glazed and slippery in the early morning dew. Busily he weaves webs to net bugs passing by.

During the day he patrols, inspecting for trapped prey. It's been a good night. A mosquito is stuck in the silky strands of his net, waiting to be breakfast. As he comes closer she thrashes to break free,

Winery and grapevines

but every flail sinks her deeper into the sticky web mesh.

"Please don't eat me," she begs. "Set me free and I'll tell you a secret."

"This better be good," he replies, "or I might eat you anyway."

"Oh, it's good. Let me loose and I'll tell you," she says. The curious arachnid yanks her free with his two hairy front legs. "Have you heard about the new bridge?" she asks.

"No, I haven't," he says, "and why should I care?"

"Because there are twice as many grapevines across the river," she says. "I flew over and saw them. The new bridge takes you right there."

He thinks this is tempting–more places to net insects. He's heard about the wild areas across the river with fewer houses. There webs are much safer from weed killers and earth movers. A new bridge could be the way to a better life. He thinks out loud, "I'll hike across with my friend. It'll be fun."

As he daydreams, the wily mosquito flits away to safety as fast as she can, determined to avoid grapevine arachnids for the rest of her life. *Until–*

Power Line Starling

It's that time of year. The starlings have already started gathering on power lines and fence posts. Sometimes hundreds at a time dot the lines between poles. Near the train depot they hold their annual convention, every once in a while swooping down to chase insect snacks. As if on cue a second string of the small birds sweeps upward and takes over the perches left vacant.

At twilight when the wind dies down, they begin working for supper in earnest. Mosquitoes are fat and juicy then too, after a day of nipping and sipping humans.

One industrious starling almost has her fill when she decides to dive one more time. Imagine her surprise when the mosquito she snatches yells, "Stop! If you eat me you'll never know my secret."

Depot, Logging and Railroad Museum

"And what's that?" the starling asks.

"Put me down and I'll tell you," she answers.

"I know a way to make your trip across the river much easier," she says. "You know how the river winds can be fierce and surprisingly gusty–and how much you love visiting the bluffs on both sides. I've seen the streaks of white droppings where you rest between trips on the old bridge. Well, now you're going to have two bridges to rest on. Soon there will be a new one south of town."

This is good news to the starling. She doesn't waste any time flying back to her flock to spread the word.

The mosquito flies away as fast as she can, determined to avoid grapevine arachnids and power line starlings for the rest of her life. *And then–*

Waterfall Frog

Up the hill on Chestnut Street behind the inn is a pond where a leopard frog has taken up lodging. At nightfall from the bedroom window overlooking the garden, you can hear his deep serenade. He often sits on a rock next to the pond waterfall, patiently waiting for insects to fly by. Then his tongue whips out and snags the unwary pests. This time it's a mosquito he aims to catch. But the mosquito spots him first and says, "Stop! I've come to tell you a secret."

The frog croaks back, "And what's that?"

"Don't eat me, and I'll tell you something that could change your life forever," the mosquito replies.

Brunswick Inn Bed and Breakfast with Restaurant

It's late and the frog bites his long tongue impatiently. "Let's hear it," he says.

"Soon there will be another way to get to the far side of the river where there are lots more mosquitoes. I've seen them. A new  bridge is being built to take you there. You won't have to swim across the treacherous river."

The frog has heard stories of others before him who started that swim and never were heard from again. "That's good to hear. Go on now, and thanks for telling me," he croaks softly. "Be sure to tell my friends in the next pond if you see them, too."

The amazing mosquito buzzes off to the neighbor's, determined to steer clear of grapevine arachnids, power line starlings and waterfall frogs for the rest of her life. *That is, until–* 

Garden Gate, Fountain and Gazebo

Elderberry Ant

Across Main Street, between the warden's museum and the old, abandoned prison building grows an elderberry bush. Just before dawn, mosquitoes munch on the bush's sweet honeydew left by insects the night before. One mosquito, unaware of a hungry ant inching closer, winces just as the ant

Warden's House and Territorial State Prison Building

grabs her leg. It breaks off! But the mosquito is okay. She can do fine on five legs. One less, though, and she might lose her balance and fall.

She scrambles to escape screaming, "Stop! I'll tell you a secret if you let me go."

"I'm too busy to listen, it better be quick. What's your silly secret, mosquito," the ant snaps.

"Have you heard about the new bridge?" the mosquito asks. "It will take you over the river where you can join other ant colonies, and life is much better," she says. "If you hurry you can get there before winter, I'm sure."

"Good idea," says the ant, and she hurries off to tell all the others on her anthill.

The amazing mosquito hobbles away to safety as quickly as she can, determined to stay away from grape-vine arachnids, power line star-lings, waterfall frogs and elder-berry ants for the rest of her life. *Of course, until–*

Cafe Damselfly

In the middle of Main Street there's a popular cafe next to the river. People meet there often for coffee, conversation, music and art, and everyone feels welcome. The damselflies think of it as an all-you-can-eat buffet. They amuse customers on the patio with their fanciful flights. There damselflies dine on insects at twilight, flitting through masses of mosquitoes, forelegs extended to wrap around their prey and devour them in mid-flight. The mosquito messenger is so heavy from sucking

humans that she barely can fly when a damselfly snatches her out of mid-air. "No, stop!" the mosquito protests, "I've come to tell you a secret. You have at the most a few months to live, and my secret will make your life so much better."

Damselfly knows her kind often doesn't live very long. There's no time to lose. "Be quick then, what is it?" she demands.

"Have you heard about the new bridge? There are hundreds more mosquitoes across the river where they don't use much pesticide," the smart little mosquito replies.

"Fabulous!" the damselfly says and takes off, iridescent blue wings all aflutter, to tell her damsel and dragonfly friends.

The mosquito promises again to stay clear of grapevine arachnids, power line starlings, waterfall frogs, elderberry ants and cafe damselflies for the rest of her life.

What ever could happen next?

Feed Mill Bat

In the tower of the feed mill, taller than any other building in Rivertown, lives a family of bats. At night they sweep the sky for mosquitoes that might fly too high. Bats are merciless hunters that use echolocation to home-in and snatch food on the fly. A brown bat can eat nearly a thousand mosquitoes each night.

"Don't eat me!" the luckless mosquito screams as she's surrounded by a bat's saber saw jaws, "I have a secret for you."

The little brown bat nose-dives to a nearby roof, spits out the mosquito and says, "What are you blabbing about?"

"Have you heard about the bridge that's being built to take bats over the

Commander Feedmill Elevator

river where there are hundreds more mosquitoes?" she breathlessly confides in a whisper. "It's being built over that hill."

The bat dashes off to broadcast the news, and the mosquito says to her self, "That was a close call." Again she resolves to avoid grapevine arachnids, power line starlings, waterfall frogs, elderberry ants, cafe damselflies and feed mill bats all the rest of her life. *It was a good plan, except for-*

Nighthawk, Whippoorwill, Chimney Swift and Barn Swallow

As soon as the sun disappears and the night insects come out, nighthawks and whippoorwills leave their retreats in the woods to exercise and find food in Rivertown. On a clear night, especially, their sharp cries can be heard–loud and staccato–piercing the quiet night sky. That, and the booming sound caused by the nighthawk's rapid rush through the air, signals mosquitoes to beware. Chimney swifts take off from the rooftops. Barn swallows, who nest under the old bridge during the day, start their insect-hunting swoops at dusk, too.

Up near the old courthouse, a swallow catching a mosquito is shocked by a scream, "Don't eat me! Or you'll never know the Rivertown secret."

The swallow spits out, "Tell me quickly if you must, I've 500 more insects to eat yet tonight."

"They're building a bridge south of town for your growing family's new nest. It's a short distance to the other shore. Over there are thousands more insects than here," the mosquito blurts out to save her life.

"Is that a fact? We'll just see," says the swallow, who instantly drops the mosquito to go check.

The mosquito pulls out of a tailspin just before

hitting the ground, and rights herself, vowing, "I'll never go anywhere near grapevine arachnids, power line starlings, waterfall frogs, elderberry ants, cafe damselflies, feed mill bats, nighthawks, whippoor-wills, chimney swifts and barn swallows again as long as I live." *Little did she know–*

County Historic Courthouse

Paddleboat Spider

There's a spider that makes her home under the old bridge. Her ancestors used to live under people's porches. It wasn't as cool in the summer and they didn't have water nearby. Under the bridge she has a drink whenever she wants. When it gets cold and snows, she's been known to hitch a ride on a boat and make her way back to shore. There are lots of spider hitchhikers on paddleboats in Rivertown. They ride around the paddle wheel like it was a Ferris wheel. It's lots of fun.

During this spider's ride on the wheel, the mosquito appears. Just before sucking her juices through nasty-looking, poison spider jaws, the mosquito blurts out, "Stop! I

Historic Lift Bridge

have a secret!"

"What?" says the spider through clenched fangs.

"Well, there's going to be a new bridge just around the bend where you can move your family," the mosquito says, pointing her needle nose. The spider knows the old bridge is getting pretty crowded with other hungry spiders competing for food. She gladly sets the mosquito free and thanks her for sharing her secret.

And the amazing mosquito mumbles an oath about never going near grapevine arachnids, power line starlings, waterfall frogs, elderberry ants, cafe damselflies, feed mill bats, nighthawks, whippoorwills, chimney swifts, barn swallows and paddleboat spiders.

River Excursion Paddleboat

Epilogue

At last, after the mosquito persuaded all her predators to move across the river, she lived happily ever after in Rivertown without them.

Across the bridge a boom town emerged. It built up fast when word got out that almost no mosquitoes lived there.

And none of this would have happened without the amazing, five-legged mosquito's bridge secret.

Lift Bridge — **Paddleboat**

Historic Courthouse — **Bookstore**

Old Prison Building — **Backstreet Doorway**

If you would like to order museum quality color prints of these and other river town images, email *scott053@tc.umn.edu* or call (651)735-4404.

Did You Know?

 **Abdomen** is another name for an insect's stomach.

 **Antennae** are long feelers on an insect's head. Mosquitoes use their antennae to explore the world around them.

 **Arachnids** are a class of eight-legged creatures that are different from true insects because arachnids don't have antennae.

 **Barn Swallows** have long, forked tails. They often fly close to the ground to catch insects.

 **Bats** are the only mammals with the power of flight. They use echolocation to locate insects.

 **Chimney Swifts** are birds that look similar to cigars with wings. They are distinguished by stiff wing movements and erratic flight. Their two wings make a crescent shape.

 **Damselflies and Dragonflies** are nicknamed "nature's helicopters" for the way they fly.

 **Leopard Frogs** with spots are the most commonly found frog in Midwestern river towns.

 **Nighthawks** can be found near rooftops in town. Their sharply pointed wings extend as long as their tails. The wings create a roar when the birds dive.

 **Proboscis** is the name for a mosquito's beak. The mosquito's very long *proboscis* is used for sucking blood to feed their young.

 **Spiders** have eight legs while mosquitoes and ants have only six. Spiders have no antennae. They are members of the arachnid class.

 **Starlings** are birds that make nests in the holes of rocks and buildings, and in hollow trees.

 **Thorax** is the chest part of an insect's body.

 **Whippoorwills** live in the woods and communicate by repeating the sound *whip-poor-weel*. They are more often heard than seen.

Word Find

Can you find these words from the story? They are hidden in the puzzle. Make a copy of this page first if you don't want to mark up your book. *(See answers on the next page.)*

whippoorwill
swallow
honeydew
mosquito
arachnid

bat
spider
frog
courthouse
paddleboat

starlings
grapevine
winery
inn
mill

depot
prison
museum
warden
chimney
swift
river
bridge
elderberry
hitchhiker
web
ant
power
line
echolocation
damselfly
dragonfly
cafe
secret
pesticides
barn
water
nighthawk
prey
predator
ran

	a	b	c	d	e	f	g	h	i	j	k	l	m	n	o	p	q	r	s	t
1	S	P	O	P	R	E	D	A	T	O	R	P	E	S	O	N	A	M	B	O
2	W	O	R	B	O	H	C	H	O	R	O	T	T	N	O	S	I	R	P	C
3	A	W	P	E	S	T	I	C	I	D	E	S	M	U	S	E	U	M	O	H
4	G	A	O	O	D	P	M	T	L	E	N	I	V	E	P	A	R	G	O	E
5	M	R	F	R	O	G	I	S	C	T	K	W	A	H	T	H	G	I	N	N
6	P	D	F	Y	I	D	N	D	O	H	A	S	O	N	I	P	I	W	E	B
7	A	E	E	R	I	V	Y	P	E	T	H	W	O	N	K	V	A	H	E	R
8	D	N	N	E	E	R	E	W	E	R	I	I	V	E	E	R	O	I	N	I
9	D	A	R	N	S	D	O	R	B	L	T	F	K	P	W	N	L	P	I	D
10	L	D	D	I	N	H	C	A	R	A	N	T	A	E	E	I	O	P	L	G
11	E	A	E	W	E	E	E	P	C	A	R	R	E	Y	R	O	L	O	R	E
12	B	M	R	O	S	Z	P	O	W	R	G	A	D	W	I	N	E	O	E	Y
13	O	S	G	M	U	O	L	O	C	C	H	E	L	O	I	N	L	R	W	L
14	A	E	D	R	O	O	P	P	O	H	W	S	W	A	L	L	O	W	O	N
15	T	L	A	V	H	S	T	A	R	L	I	N	G	S	I	S	B	I	P	N
16	U	F	B	C	T	L	Q	R	A	G	Y	M	N	M	O	T	B	L	Y	I
17	D	L	E	A	R	O	V	U	A	N	N	A	N	O	S	A	R	L	E	J
18	O	Y	K	F	U	B	A	R	I	I	E	L	D	E	R	B	E	R	R	Y
19	R	A	N	E	O	L	L	A	M	T	N	A	A	N	Y	G	M	N	P	O
20	S	A	Z	U	C	Q	Y	L	F	N	O	G	A	R	D	I	O	Z	Z	R

Word Find Solutions

These are the answers to the puzzle on the previous page.

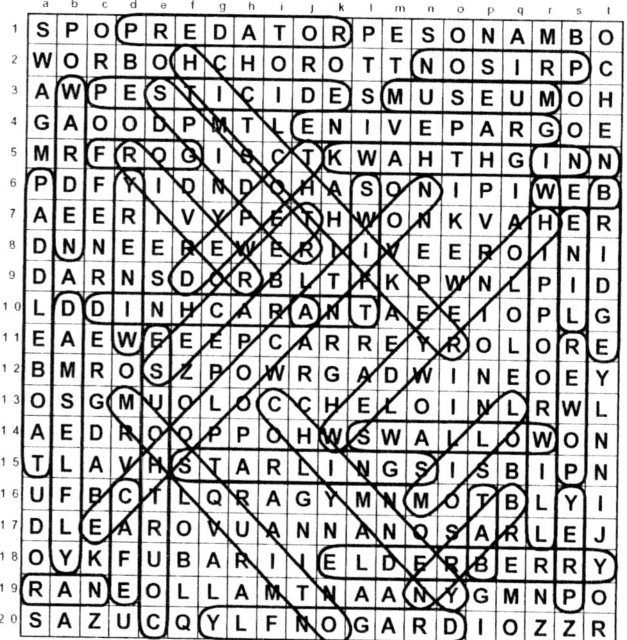

About the Author

Jane Beecher Scott has been shooting photographs of Rivertown for more than a year. Not ordinary photos–these look more like Impressionist oil paintings. They illustrate the pages of this book.

To make them, she shot instant-process film with an old-fashioned camera from the 1950s. After shooting the photo while the film developed she rubbed the surface of it with a pointed tool quickly before it finished developing. When she became a new grandmother, she decided to write this book for her grandchild and use her Rivertown photographs for illustrations.

For inspiration she propped up the photos inside her studio so she could look at them everyday and then let her imagination go to work. At the same time there was a new-bridge debate in the river town

near her home. That became the theme for the story. The next step was to decide on a main character, the mosquito. Then she asked herself, "What are other creatures in the mosquito's life, and where might these creatures be found?" That's how the bats in the feed mill tower, whippoorwills and swallows by the old courthouse, waterfall frogs in the inn's pond, and elderberry ants near the old prison building came to be. But that's another story.

She took the photo of the prison building a week before it burned down. It was a terrible thing that happened to this important historic landmark from 1890. She'd already put the photo in the book but had some doubts about keeping it because it might make readers feel sad. Someone said, "No leave it. It will be a memory that those who remember it will treasure." So the prison picture stayed.

Beecher Scott continues to create Impressionist-like photographic images. She also teaches at a community college and runs an independent consulting business.